cat
Katze

rabbit

Hase

**dog**

Hund

**chick**

**Küken**

duck
Ente

**sheep**

**Schaf**

goat
Ziege

**pig**

Schwein

# donkey

Esel

**horse**

**Pferd**

# cow

## Kuh

mouse

Maus

**bat**

Fledermaus

bee

Biene

**spider**

Spinne

**fox**

**Fuchs**

**deer**

Hirsch

# squirrel

**Eichhörnchen**

# hedgehog

## Igel

# owl

Eule

# frog

**Frosch**

**snake**

Schlange

# racoon

## Waschbär

# parrot

## Papagei

**toucan**

**tukan**

**alligator**

alligator

**sea turtle**

**meeresschildkröte**

# flamingo

**Flamingo**

# penguin

**Pinguin**

crab

Krabbe

**jellyfish**

Qualle

# seal

**Robbe**

# shark

## Hai

# whale

## Wal

**orca**

Orca

starfish
Seestern

# rhinoceros

## Nashorn

**panda**

Panda

# monkey

## Affe

# lion

## Löwe

tiger

**Tiger**

**elephant**

**Elefant**